About the Author

LAURA HAWRYLUCK received her MD from the University of Western Ontario where she served her Internal Medicine residency. She completed a Fellowship in Critical Care at the University of Manitoba and an MSc. in Bioethics from the University of Toronto, Canada. Professor of Critical Care Medicine at the University of Toronto, she was awarded the Queen's Golden Jubilee Medal for contributions to Canada in improving end of life care, the Medico-Legal Society of Toronto award for contributions to medicine and law, and the University of Toronto Interdepartmental Critical Care Medicine Humanitarian Award for her contributions to international humanitarian work. She is the author of two other poetry books "An ICU Doctor's Reflections" and "Words that Matter" published by Olympia Publishers.

ICU Pandemic Diary

Dr. Laura A. Hawryluck

ICU Pandemic Diary

Olympia Publishers
London

www.olympiapublishers.com
OLYMPIA PAPERBACK EDITION

Copyright © Dr. Laura A. Hawryluck 2022
©Cover illustration be Ramya Satyanarayana RN

The right of Dr. Laura A. Hawryluck to be identified as author of this work has been asserted in accordance with sections 77 and 78 of the Copyright, Designs and Patents Act 1988.

All Rights Reserved

No reproduction, copy or transmission of this publication may be made without written permission.
No paragraph of this publication may be reproduced, copied or transmitted save with the written permission of the publisher, or in accordance with the provisions
of the Copyright Act 1956 (as amended).

Any person who commits any unauthorized act in relation to this publication may be liable to criminal prosecution and civil claims for damage.

A CIP catalogue record for this title is available from the British Library.

ISBN: 978-1-80074-777-7

This is a work of fiction.
Names, characters, places and incidents originate from the writer's imagination. Any resemblance to actual persons, living or dead, is purely coincidental.

First Published in 2022

Olympia Publishers
Tallis House
2 Tallis Street
London
EC4Y 0AB

Printed in Great Britain

Dedication

For Dean, Nathan, Mervyn, Jeroen and Tex. Thank you for the last moments of laughter before our worlds changed. Those precious memories helped me get through the darkest times.

For Ramya. Thank you for always being there throughout all of this and so much more, and for always brightening my life.

For Rima. Thank you for all your unwavering support and laughing with me through thick and thin. It means the world.

For my Toronto Western Hospital MSNICU family. Know that there are simply not enough words to thank each and every one of you.

Acknowledgements

Thank you to my family and all my close friends – you know who you are – for all your loving support throughout this very challenging time, for understanding, for listening, for really being there in the times when I wasn't so strong. Know that I will never forget and that it means more than I can ever express. I want to extend a very special thank you to a truly awesome friend Ramya Satyanarayana an incredible ICU RN who defines kindness, caring and advocacy, for sharing her beautiful art to grace the cover of this book. I hope my words have done justice to her beautiful gift and tremendous talent. I want to thank my Toronto Western Hospital MSNICU family for their passion in caring for those who need our help and their ingenuity and courage in overcoming significant challenges every single day. You are all incredible. Thank you to my friends at both the CBC and BBC whose honest and accurate reporting has shone a light on what critically ill people and their families have been through during this continuing pandemic and what our journey as ICU healthcare professionals with them has been like. Thank you to my entire team at Olympia for believing in me, for believing that poetry can capture moments lived in the ICU: the heartbreak and the hope that never leaves us.

Introduction

This book seeks once again to open the doors of the ICUs, this time as teams confront the frontline of the devastating COVID-19 pandemic. I wrote it to describe what it was really like, to capture the emotions and stressors, the things that went well and the impact on ICU teams when things went terribly wrong. The moments captured are not all that we lived. They are the moments that truly stood out. If there is a rawness about them, this is because it's an honest depiction of what happened. May we never forget. May we learn. May we heal.

Without a Name

Initially without a name,
Emerging all the same,
Speed of light spread,
Deep anticipatory dread,
Fear running through your head;
News footage of so, so many dead.

COVID-19 it became.
The world, not the same.
Countries in a panic,
Crashing with so many sick,
The start of lockdowns,
Eerie silence, empty streets all around,
Isolation within, desolation without.

Droplet or airborne?
So many unknowns;
Worldwide shortages of PPE;
Compromised protection of me from you,
Of you from me,
Worldwide shortages of ventilators and drugs,
Now how can that be?
Rationed N95,
Will there be enough to keep us alive?
Possibly recycling shields and masks,

Is there such a task?

Predictions never seen,
A story that has never been,
Home to hospital,
Hospital to home,
No one about,
You don't go out,
Today five admissions and more tomorrow,
Only the start of so much sorrow.

Will we get through this alive?
When will we all see the other side?

Sentinels at the Door

The hospital doors are firmly closed,
Guarded by re-deployed sentinels;
Masked, behind glass.
A monotony of screening questions,
Reminders of the narrowness of life,
In its current conception.

Any headache, fever, cough?
Any travel?
Any sick contacts at all?
Every day the same greeting at the door,
No less, no more.

Next, a journey to the scrub machine,
More battered and tattered than you would dream.
Will it be a good day?
Will I win the scrub lottery today?
Distance from scrub to slot machine,
Narrower than it would seem.

Scrubs, cap and mask;
Already a feeling of suffocation, don't ask;
A walk to the ICU
To see what is happening with you;
The hall a tunnel to COVID's destruction,

Ironically, under construction.

A day trying to keep people alive,
As more and more and more arrive.
So tired and so thirsty under the visor, the mask,
Though a question now no one asks,
Way past midnight the struggles wage,
This virus, the plague of our age.

Finally home, to bed I crash.
Destroyed and heartbroken
Though no one asks.
Sleep for three or four hours of rest,
No more, and, if lucky, no less.

Any headache, fever, cough?
Any travel?
Any sick contacts at all?
Every day the same greeting at the door,
No less, no more.

Pandemic ICU

When it all began,
The headlines ran,
Lower mortality than the flu.
I believed it was true,
Didn't you?

So many ill,
So many dead,
Research sure,
Improvements… but no cure,
Vaccines, yes;
How the virus will mutate still,
Anyone's guess;
And no one knows what lies ahead.

Once again, I don scrubs,
Cap, mask, shield, gown and gloves,
Who I am concealed;
Eyes inscrutable through my shield.
We watch each other through the glass;
You also in a mask;
Can you breathe long enough to last?
Hands in gloves,
Glass door opens with a shove.

A few short hours ago,
You were coughing, couldn't breathe.
Initially a little oxygen was enough for it to slow,
Put you at ease.

In a few more hours, your chest burned.
Your problems breathing returned.
The team got you to self-prone,
Skills in teaching how, well-honed.
This helped for a while.
You are even able to text, to smile.
Yet illness' march relentless;
Gasping again;
High flow oxygen, team doing all they can.
Trying to show what you are made of,
It's not enough.

Your gaze steady on mine,
When I explain there is not much time.
As the rest of the ICU team prepares,
Gathers their tools and medications with care.
Last video calls to those you love,
Have you forgotten anyone? Think.
Time is up – in a blink.

Hands in gloves held tight,
Eyes bright,
Courage in the face of fright;
Now we are ready to sedate,
To intubate.

Blood gases analyzed.
You will need to be paralyzed,
And once again proned,
Through tubes and equipment, flipped,
A skill the team has honed,
A position assumed quick.

Hands in gloves,
Glass door opened with a shove.
Removal of PPE,
Though enough remains,
That no one can really see me.
I pick up the phone,
Outwardly contained,
Yet feeling isolated and alone.
I tell them everything went fine.
We now just need to wait and see,
In time.

A Doctor in a Pandemic

On the outside looking in,
Is where I have always been.
Years of study, buried deep, never fitting in;
Disappearing even more for exams;
Friends wondering where I have been,
Wondering where I am.

On the outside looking in,
Seeing people gather,
Like nothing else in the world matters,
Except maybe that next lager.
Watching, with longing,
Wondering at their effortless sense of belonging.

On the outside looking in,
Seeing scenes I used to so love,
Now those I wouldn't want to approach,
Risks I wouldn't want to broach,
Even with mask and gloves.
Don't they know viral variants abound;
That it's in the air, all around?

On the outside looking in,
In a future place and time,
I close my eyes but in my mind,

I can see you,
Now… in the ICU.
The laughter has stopped.
Your family is watching the clock.
Waiting for an update,
Wondering where I am,
Struggling to understand.

The Arrivals

First it was the elderly, the old,
From Long Term Care;
COVID spread like a wildfire, brazen and bold;
Brought in by those who care;
Scorching and burning all there.

In through the emergency doors, they poured.
Those left behind,
Abandoned,
Ignored.

Quickly they filled the ICU,
With CXRs that shocked more than a few.
Some Happy in Hypoxia,
As they risked horrific brain anoxia.
Others confused and agitated,
With an urgent need to be sedated.

Oxygen saturations falling off a cliff,
No one could believe this.
Recovery not as swift.
An ICU breathtaking wait.
How long will it take?
When do we need to intubate?
Hesitate,

Will it abate?

An intubated struggle desperately ensued.
A sense of worry and hopelessness, deep, deep in the ICU;
Despite the awful predictions,
Many, many survived.
When those far, far younger died…

No Visitors Allowed

The ICU is both busy and quiet.
Patients are heavily sedated and paralyzed;
The whole environment heavily sterilized.

Only eyes revealed,
Through masks and shields.
It's hard to hear;
HEPA filters present, loud and clear.

Access denied.
No families allowed inside.
By Ministry decrees,
Reinforced by tough hospital policies.
Unless the person you love is dying,
Unless you can't see or speak for crying.

Unaware;
Patients who can't share,
Who they are, what matters;
Little time for families to chatter;
Despair,
So many calls to make,
Never a moment's break.

Sclerotic;

Work hypnotic;
In the loss of humanity, now robotic.
Robbed,
Of who we are,
Of what matters,
Of how we care.

Too Young

They were young.
Out and about,
Laughing in the face of the sun,
And having so much fun.

Patios and beaches,
Closed for so long,
Then, like a mirage,
All restrictions gone.

Don't you remember
What it was like to be young,
After a long, long December?

To fete, to sing,
Celebrate all life can bring.
Never thinking your song can be sung.

Not a vaccine among them,
Didn't qualify,
And many shunned them.
It's just a flu.
There will be no need for ICU.
Too young for the shot;
Not too young to die, to rot.

Essential

It was essential you worked,
Bills to pay,
A little one on the way.
Crowded conditions,
Only a thin mask for protection.

It started with headaches,
Then a cough,
No way to take time off.
Then you couldn't breathe,
Still, you tried not to believe;
Soon you were in the ICU,
Soon you needed a tube.

Pundits declared
You would still be able to breathe,
If only you had Paid Sick Leave.
Such opinions bandied wide and quick;
But *why* did you even have to get sick??

The campaign was loud and widespread,
Even as through your family the virus spread,
Putting them in the hospital too;
Some even in the ICU,
Next to you.

And the ICU wondered
Where was the care before the fall?
Why did you have to get sick at all??
Why wasn't the loudly-hailed intervention
Not near-total prevention?

Around the world, amiss
Overcrowded workplaces still exist.
The virus has clearly shown us this.
Such poorly filtered air,
Yet no one who cares.

Whole families vanished,
In a viral vanquish.
The safest workplace,
Shouldn't this be the point of grace?

Unvaccinated

Hidden, far more than shown,
Wild fear of the unknown.
Hesitancy… standing on the edge of a cliff;
A balance of risks;
A serious miscalculation,
In this equation.

Clear, a weakness down one side;
Wild fear of what's inside;
Hospital… lying on a CT table;
A balance unstable;
A variant of concern,
In conflagration, burns.

A large clot,
A major artery blocked.
Clear swelling in the brain;
Intubated.
Sedated.

Hidden, far more than shown,
Wild fear of the future unknown;
Forever altered.
Forever changed.
If you had known it could lead to this…
What if?

Afraid

Issues of mental health;
You barely even liked yourself;
Another needle in your arm;
Really, what's the harm?

A more sedentary life;
Work from home, no struggles or strife;
Sudden onset of shortness of breath;
It will go away, surely, if only you rest.

Isolated and alone;
No one else at home;
No friends phone;
Who will miss you when you're gone?

A new lump in your breast;
Noticed as you undress;
Now lumps under your arm;
You will wait, what's the harm?

As the virus rampages,
Accrued collateral damages;
These stories
And more besides
Avoid the hospital my dear;

COVID is spreading don't you hear?

In the ER,
As I gaze from afar,
You are all undergoing CPR.
Afraid to seek help needed;
Ignoring warnings that should have been heeded.

Avoid the hospital my dear;
COVID is spreading don't you hear?

Braced[1]

I hear the phone's rings,
Braced for the fear it brings.
I call from the ICU,
Braced, for the news I have to share with you.

I really wish I didn't need to phone.
I really wish I could tell you he is coming home.
Now… your voice is on the line;
Right away you **know** nothing is fine.
Sheer, horrifying dread,
Doctor… Is he dead?

I try to keep my voice from breaking,
Though my heart is shredded and aching.
As you cry,
Know my own eyes are **far** from dry.
Clutching the phone, white knuckled,
Knees buckled,
Someone brings me a chair;
So I don't fall into thin air.

---

[1] Originally published in ICU Management &Practice. Citation: Hawryluck L, Styra R., Mental Health in the Ongoing Pandemic: How will we be Okay? ICU Management & Practice, 21(2):78 — 82. Used with Permission.

Comfort I try to bring,
As the ICU phones continue their infernal ring.
There are others on their way.
Somehow… I need to get through the rest of my day.
No words.
Grief deferred.

Twice a Day

Every day I go to work with a heavy heart.
So many sick, so many dying;
A bolt of lightning from the sky;
NO! the heart wrenching cry,
But positive swabs don't lie.
The roar of thunder,
As the virus rips families asunder.

Twice a day I know the time.
Like clockwork, it starts on a dime.
Clanging pots and pans;
Clapping hands;
Bursts of song;
From balconies for miles long.

Clapping and clanging,
For healthcare "heroes" it's meant to be;
But that certainly doesn't feel like me.
Cause to reflect,
So very far from perfect;
So many people we can't stop from dying;
So many people we can't stop from crying.

Thank yous and Hoorahs;
Clapping and clanging;

Speed the way in,
Warm the way back out.

A ROAR beyond shouts;
Not all Heroes wear capes.
But even those uneasy,
And even those "heroes" but briefly,
Try to help others escape,
Unspeakable fates.

The Gifts

Day to day,
Night to night,
Shift to shift,
Life… an existence of just this.

From home to hospital,
From hospital to home,
Never do roam;
Dead on your feet;
When did you last eat?

No food… even in your house;
Just… creepily, the scratching of a mouse.
When out of the blue,
Miraculously, food in the ICU,
An out-of-work chef's donation,
A life-saving, unexpected viral ration.

A *very* precious gift;
More than just food,
A total change of mood;
Someone, strangers unknown, care.
Someone – for us – really is out there.

Once again home;

In its silence, all alone;
A need for basic provisions;
Yet so many inhibitions.

Given special status,
For some, a status non-gratis,
For others, ahead of the line,
A moment stolen in time;
First access to the essential stores,
Who could ever ask for more?
Yet really… why should we be first through the doors?

No matter what the future may bring,
No matter if it cries or sings,
We will always remember moments like this;
From those who could scarcely afford such gifts.

Remaining Light

Every night,
In the darkness of the remaining light,
I return home.
Some nights,
I get to turn off the phone;
My time, my own.

Every night,
I try to hide,
As I unpack the deep inside;
The tears, the worries,
The stress, the rage,
Writ large across my page.

Every night,
I tear down the walls, the divides
That separate me from the day's events;
The true awful that bears no public comment.

Every night,
I re-become me;
Or, at least as close as I can be,
Before I crash into bed,
To get the ghostly echoes out of my head.

Every morning,
I must rebuild the walls,
Farther and farther down narrowing halls;
So I can once again withstand
Tragedies that I don't understand.
And to worried family and friends,
One day… I will make amends.

The News

I no longer watch the news;
Stories of overflowing hospitals and ICUs;
Endless closely-packed masses
Protesting social distancing and masks;
Endless data, graphs and charts;
Endless speculation on how did it start;
Man-made or Nature's art?

High above, spinning, spinning, spinning overhead,
From tropical storm;
To funnel cloud formed;
Down below, lives smashed and disrupted;
With each news cycle turned,
Nero watching, while Rome burned.

Every shot captured drama;
Becomes a new trauma;
More coming at me, I cannot withstand;
An ostrich in the sand;
More coming from me, you can't demand;

Deep in the churned debris of its path,
I try to piece together the pieces of its wrath
Man-made or Nature's Art?
Instead of how did it start,
Tell me… how long will it last?

Resilience

When the winds are mean,
And the world is as dark as it seems,
Where do you find the resilience to go on?
When all the light is gone…
When it seems there will never be a dawn…

How do you become the sword pulled from the rock?
Find your way from the waves onto the dock?
Find the cool well deep, deep inside?
Reach into where inner strength resides?

Acknowledge the emotions,
The upheavals and commotions;
The inner turmoil,
In which your mind roils;
Their eddies and pools are reflections of you,
Insights into how you grew…

How do you pick yourself up from today's sorrows,
And know you will be stronger tomorrow?
To be human is to feel,
To be a leader is to reveal,
How – exactly – you heal.

Retired?

A career, a life devoted for;
Gave 'til there was no more.
Started a new chapter and verse,
A need to rest, to no longer rehearse.
Great performances at an end,
Thank yous and goodbyes, forever friends.

As the ICUs filled to overflow,
Calls for those retired answered in droves;
Knowledge and skills can't replace,
Pleas for help as ICUs expanded their space;
Though peace well-earned,
'Til the end, forever friends.

Yet despite media reports,
Of ease
To return to ICUs
If you please;
Regulatory bodies and red tape,
Questions
Of past best date?
Police background investigations,
Questions
Of worth
Sometimes… a path shouldn't be reversed.

Yet the imprint of ICU,
Diecast,
Chiseled and carved over years, never past;
Marred,
Now who you are;
Even if left clinical practice five or more years ago,
Quick to remember what you know
Help needed,
Calls heeded,
In the end, often not pursued or denied;
Even as people died.

The Numbers

The numbers are up,
The numbers are down,
In the stories that abound,
Many truths are found.
Life is a roller coaster,
And… this is far from over.

One lockdown after another,
As the whole world shudders,
ICU numbers lag behind and build,
Virus' promises now fulfilled.
Behind its heavy closed doors,
A terrible score,
The stories of the poor;
And… around the world,
Swirl and find,
Tragedies that bind.

Essential issues not addressed;
Pervasive sins of greed not confessed;
Problems denied.
Critics sidelined.
Hard intensive work not done,
As many see the setting of the sun.
This is not an elderly disease,

This is not a "blue collar" disease,
Wherein others are licensed to do as they please.
There must be a greater repair;
Hear the warnings in its scare.

Joy as numbers fall;
The ICU still fighting death's call.
Asking, why can you not hear the virus' siren call?
All it awaits is a change in the weather;
All it awaits is your next get-together;
For its next wave…
Who then… will be saved?

Birds in the Sky

The rattle and hum
Draws all eyes on high.
The color of the bird?
Orange[2], in the sky.
It's meaning rendering numb,
Now… where did this bird come from?

Over two thousand patient transfers and still counting;
Spread of viral pandemic sickness,
The toll of life-threatening illness,
The toll of grief still mounting,
Hundreds of kilometers from home
And all alone;
With fright seized,
Struggling to breathe.

So far from family and friends,
Will you ever see home again?
How will it end?
What will happen if you die?
And still that orange 'copter flies
Across cloudless sunny skies.

---

[2] In Ontario, Canada, critical care land or air transportation between hospitals is handled by the provincial ORNGE organization. Their helicopters are painted in a distinctive orange color.

While down below,
Scents of lilacs on the wind,
The blooms of spring,
The real birds still sing;
And still people look way up on high
And sigh.

ICU Triage

Who will live and who will die?
For this I can't look to the sky.
For this terrible choice you see,
Rests with me.

How can I be asked to choose
Who will win and who will lose?
When the music stops,
Fate is now locked.
Who will get a chair?
Who will have to climb the holy stairs?

In this virus' advance,
It's a tangled and awful dance,
There are no heroes,
There is no romance.

To make the most horrifying decisions,
Is there any real precision?
The haunting, hollow choice rests with I;
Who will live… and who will die?

The Hoax

The pandemic is a hoax,
By "doctors" stoked.
A search for power and ascension,
Stardom and media attention.

Nothing but misdirection,
There is no virus there.
Storm the hospitals,
Take the dare.

Any excuse to lockdown,
To bring our economy to a meltdown.
And just let us ask
Who can *breathe* through these masks?
There is no virus to be found.
It's only a conspiracy all around.
Take back our lives
How else will we survive?

The way out of this mess?
mRNA vaccines
Completely obscene;
Full of microchips to control our minds,
What else will we find?
Interfering with our DNA, confess;

And magnetic features now possessed.
Spoons to nose, keys to neck,
Did they think we wouldn't check?

Let loose from a lab,
On us to keep tabs.
Protests everywhere abound;
Evil doctors and politicians must be found.
Power to social media takedowns;
Anger building in the towns.

Danger's clarions sound;
Reality inside out, upside down;
Halls of menace and shattered mirrors;
Perilous paths ever nearer;
Ways from lies to truths, no clearer;
Price paid ever dearer.

Behind the Mask

Snaking around cheeks and necks,
Weeping wounds crust over,
Ripped open when the night is over.
Apparently a "Hero", thankfully never a Saint,
N95 Warrior paint,
Trying to ignore people's selfish taint.
Yet... ire,
As they light their perverted bonfires.

Politicians, kings of the realm,
Supposedly at the helm,
Others in command,
But it's only sleight of hand;
Vacationing on the sly,
For them, you see, rules never apply.
And, in the face of science, they fly.
As my face falls apart,
See the scars across my heart,
That will always leave a mark.

Battered faith in human nature,
Can you picture
The stories I can't tell
From the Frontlines of Hell?
As I fall to my knees,

Ask me is there anything in which I still believe.
Cut down.
Without a sound.

What's it like you ask,
For all "Heroes" behind the mask?
Do you see our pain,
Through the escalating rain,
When memories of love are all that remain?
Do you see me cry?
Can you look me in the eye?
Do you still see the cracks,
As you watch our hearts turn to stone?
Cut down.
No longer without a sound.

Still Here

The moment I stop moving,
I slip into sleep.
I have been in the ICU, buried so deep.
So tired, I can barely stand on my feet.

As I look all around,
Alarms constantly sound.
People rushing here and there,
Yet another person in need of care.
Where are we going to put them?
How can we re-arrange?
Thankfully to us, such questions are far from strange.

While we are all nearly falling off our feet,
Despite the near-overwhelming media hysteria,
And our hold on resources so precarious;
Despite the storm of emotional tweets,
About the failure to cope,
The loss of hope,
That supposedly grips us in its sweep,
I don't see complete burnout all around.
These claims are not – at their heart – sound.

The facts are the team is, at its core, still calm.
Our knowledge of / care for each other, a balm.

Yes, we are strained.
Yes, with our patients and families we feel so much pain.
Yet, defiantly, we still reign.

Know we are still here.
We will always be here.
This is what we do.
This is the ICU.

Aftermath

I stand alone in the empty room;
Equipment off,
You can hear a pin drop;
Bed sheets clean, calm, pulled tight;
Hospital corners, not a wrinkle in sight;
My fingers gently touch the linen so cool;
Images burn on a continuous spool.

Doc, I am going to beat this... you will see—words when we first met,
Play in my head their constant refrain;
Doc, I can see you're worried... but you will be surprised,
As you held my hand and looked deep in my eyes,
I don't want them to worry—words before we had to intubate;
Encouraged to call your family anyway,
Before we had to heavily sedate.

The struggle—the hope as from the abyss, you appeared to gain ground;
Only to lose it again and more;
Just when we thought you were winning—was when we didn't know the score;
All marked by the ventilator's and monitors' screams;
All muffled by the incessant HEPA filter roars.

Clean, calm sheets pulled tight;
Not a wrinkle in sight;
The quiet deafening now in the near night;
I fight back the images with all my might;
My throat stings with tears;
Yet they well... and sobs are so very near.

To not disturb the peace,
I step back and quietly close the door.
At the moment, I am not needed here anymore;
If only I could leave behind the images, the constant refrains;
Doc, I will beat this – said with *every, single, labored* breath;
Well... you *did* give it your best...
If only I could leave behind the images, the constant refrains;
I will never be the same.

Re-Deployed

In the days and nights without end,
You came and helped our service extend.
You didn't really know us,
Yet entered our world without fuss,
Pitched in without question,
With barely a raised eyebrow or change in expression.
Learned our foibles, our practice, our ways,
Helped us through the fog, through the haze.

From different backgrounds and skills,
Bringing your own instincts to care for those so ill.
You incredibly appeared,
With courage and cheer.
You worked with heart,
Of our ICU family, became a part.
In the face of illness so severe,
Your willingness to help so sincere,
You lifted us all;
You helped us stand tall.

As this virus' wave now comes to its end,
We realize how much on you we have come to depend;
How you have become fast friends.
But… though the ICU is still overflowing,
You are told it's time to be going.

To return,
To your own field learned,
And that for which you yearn.
For others now need care,
And they need you there.

Somehow we must carry on,
Through days and nights so long,
For the ICU has no end;
Sadly we must bid "au revoir" my friends.
I will see you as you were once more.
I will hope for the day this all becomes lore.

We will have to make do.
We will see the rest of it through,
Still here… in the ICU.
No words at all remain except
This very simple refrain
Thank you,
Thank you,
Thank you.

End of a Wave

Instead of a wave cresting above,
We step out
Of gowns and gloves,
Of shields and masks,
More free at last;
A viral lull,
ICUs no longer over full.

Of us, what has become?
We have lost some.
Other hearts are just numb.
Some have become undone.
All of us are more blind;
Some, hope will never find;

A dragging exhaustion,
Horrors never forgotten;
A deep depression,
So many awful losses;
A sinking panic,
Routine tasks now complex arithmetic;
Things we used to do,
Now enjoyed by only a few.

Variants still rise,

No longer any surprise;
Dread of another wave,
Houses of cards cave...

The Disconnect

All of a sudden the world moves on,
As though all its troubles are gone,
Over... faster than your favorite song.
Left behind,
Those who can't make any sign,
Those who no longer belong.

Summer is here in all its glory,
A worldwide signal for a different story.
The messaging has changed,
Optimism – false? – reigns.

It must be getting so much better too
For all of you in the ICU.
Comments well meant,
Landing on teams spent.

A hope that seems fanciful,
The reality inescapable,
The disconnect even laughable,
Building isolation palpable.

The ICU
Is in the business of rescue.
The pressures not eased,

Now only increased.
A strain that grows,
And it's starting to show.
COVID-19 has not cleared,
People are still losing those held dear.

The ICU
Is facing what is also true,
Backlogs must be cleared.
Don't you hear?
Surgeries long delayed,
Now the piper must be paid;
And… maybe yet another wave.
No relief in sight,
Only the continuation of long, never-ending night.

No break,
Nothing to celebrate;
No time to recuperate;
Teams fighting waves of despair.
Does no one care?
A simple need for air.

It must be getting so much better too
For all of you in the ICU.
Comments well meant,
Land on shoulders already so bent.
Tone deaf, though well-meaning in intent;
The public response… the shadow of a smile;
Maybe… In a while.

... And the Next Wave

From a distance, we watch the numbers rise,
With something akin to despair, not surprise;
Like a train barreling with certainty to its last station,
Living up to its studied reputation,
Yet obscured with smoke, myths and lies,
Clarity wrought only in its final demise.

From a distance we watch the numbers rise,
With something akin to fear,
At risk, everything in life held dear.
From behind our masks,
The cold realization that past is not past;
From behind our eyes,
Haunting images, still fresh, also rise.

From a distance, we watch the turn to exponential growth;
Many begin to question the nature of an Oath;
Still others, the nature of persistence;
The issue of a calling v. that of a kinder existence;
As the train nears its destination,
Its very last station,
Wounds that are deep tears,
Cannot, with certainty, be repaired.

Fires of variants of concern;

We watch, as communities burn;
Global openings cannot be reconciled;
The Greek alphabet, a brainchild defiled;
Majestic, now reviled;
Each hitting younger and younger;
Now, the innocence of children going under.

Distance is covered so very fast;
No longer watching, now aghast;
With something akin to dismay we grieve;
Vanished, any reprieve;
With something akin to horror
We cross yet another border;
Behind our eyes,
New nightmares prise
Any remaining semblance of public guise;
The train has arrived.

Mandatory Vaccines

Does it ever seem
That we thrive more on man-made controversies
Than on dreams?

Placards raised;
Talks of rights and freedoms ablaze;
Yet rights do not draw breath, my friend,
To responsibilities upend.

Live and learn;
Watch the masses storm and anger churn;
Each protest, a larger mass;
Each protest, a pandemic more steadfast.

If we thrived more on dreams,
We would lead with mandatory vaccines;
The arc of discovery and responsibility align,
For there to be real freedom for all in our time.

To My ICU Family

The first time I stepped into the ICU
Wide-eyed,
I was terrified;
Slowly I realized,
Though demanding,
Often beyond any outside understanding,
It was the field I loved
Like a hand in a comfortable glove.

There were days heavy with disaster;
Days full of undiluted joy… and even laughter;
Days when I was driven to the brink,
But whenever I stopped to think,
There was never any place I would rather be
…are you beginning to see?

A truth spoken
All for one,
And one for all;
For those in need,
To prevent a precipitous fall;
Slowly I realized,
Out of the ICU you could take me,
But the ICU could not be extracted from me.
… now can you see?

But now something is broken inside,
Anxious and depressed,
Way beyond stressed,
At the smallest request,
Horrors I see every time I close my eyes,
Emotions rattle around I can no longer hide.

I have always been so strong.
But now… something is so very wrong.
I can't sleep,
I feel I am in way too deep,
I *am* strong.
But I… I can no longer go on.
… now what do you see?

I am trying not to feel small;
I *know* that I have given it my all.
To my ICU family,
I… I… I *have* to leave.
Know that my love for you will always run deep,
And in my heart you will always be.
Tell me please… tell me you will always *see*
… me

We Will Outlast

A spiky virus spins lives awry.
The loss of those held so dear;
The loss of dreams, and futures no longer clear;
Through so many masks and across distances we cry.
So many lives on standby,
So many people just trying to get by;
The fears of getting ill,
And no cures… still.

Yet reasons for hope and optimism exist
Within this darkest of midst.
From the ICU hell zone,
Where the ravages of the virus call home,
From the depth of the PPE,
That separates you from me,
I know this is true.
I have emerged to say
Better days are on the way.

Listen to what I have seen,
The insights I have gleaned.
The pandemic that haunts us all,
Has broken down hospital walls;
Knitted tighter team bonds within its halls.
Re-deployed people and equipment built understanding;

Toppled egos and siloes longstanding;
Created new approaches for better care
That previously would not have been dared.

New monitoring devices to prevent illness' slide,
New ventilators to expand available bedsides,
Mobile ICUs and ORs from shipping containers modified,
New data, projections and graphs,
So that no one slips through help's grasp.
And so many new vaccines,
Developed at a breakneck pace no one had ever seen.
Add new research platforms applied,
To keep you and I alive
To allow us once again to thrive.

Instead of technologies so smart,
Drawing us in, driving us apart,
Now they are used with vision
Quelling our divisions.
Concerts that help us take isolation in some stride,
New ways of fundraising for good causes with pride,
No longer struggling alone and apart
Bringing us together, heart to heart.

Forced to discard stability,
And even every measure of tranquility,
United in quests for new possibilities,
For each of us to have new utility,
Discoveries of new abilities,
Of untapped capabilities,
New means of creative expression

That help stave off depression;
Parodies that make us laugh,
Promise a better time within our grasp.
All would never have been known
Had this pandemic not roamed.

A need for gentleness to rule the land,
An urgent call to help whoever you can,
Life to its fundamentals distilled,
The rejection of needless thrills,
The rejection of all things shrill,
For far too many tears have been spilled,
For us not to find the will,
To always show humanity,
And generosity;
For us not to see
Not only you and me, but we.

Because all this is true
The world will be made better anew
Know that even behind the masks
We will outlast.

What Have We Learned?

What have we learned?
After 2020, 2021 and 2022 records are burned,

Soon it will be 2023s turn
Beyond a shadow of a doubt,
What will ring out?

It *is* a small world after all.
Disney was right.
Celebrate and protect one and all;
Do not take fright.

Some rules should never be broken.
Some thoughts and words, never spoken.
Don't judge a person by the mask on their face;
Look deeper at how they use their social media space.

Learn to focus on the eyes.
Read the secrets they keep.
Rarer are the lies;
See the happiness you seek.

Know we are more the same.
Learn to acknowledge each other's pains.
Work *together* to effect change.
Be kind.
In this world there really is too little time.

Most "heroes" will be forever unsung.
All are still heroes even if now undone